Putting on a Play

by Claire Daniel
illustrated by Nancy Poydar

Harcourt
SCHOOL PUBLISHERS

Copyright © by Harcourt, Inc.

All rights reserved. No part of this publication may be reproduced or transmitted in any form or by any means, electronic or mechanical, including photocopy, recording, or any information storage and retrieval system, without permission in writing from the publisher.

Requests for permission to make copies of any part of the work should be addressed to School Permissions and Copyrights, Harcourt, Inc., 6277 Sea Harbor Drive, Orlando, Florida 32887–6777. Fax: 407-345-2418.

HARCOURT and the Harcourt Logo are trademarks of Harcourt, Inc., registered in the United States of America and/or other jurisdictions.

Printed in Mexico

ISBN 10: 0-15-350275-4
ISBN 13: 978-0-15-350275-0

Ordering Options
ISBN 10: 0-15-349940-0 (Grade 5 ELL Collection)
ISBN 13: 978-0-15-349940-1 (Grade 5 ELL Collection)
ISBN 10: 0-15-357310-4 (package of 5)
ISBN 13: 978-0-15-357310-1 (package of 5)

> If you have received these materials as examination copies free of charge, Harcourt School Publishers retains title to the materials and they may not be resold. Resale of examination copies is strictly prohibited and is illegal.

> Possession of this publication in print format does not entitle users to convert this publication, or any portion of it, into electronic format.

2 3 4 5 6 7 8 9 10   126   12 11 10 09 08 07

Characters

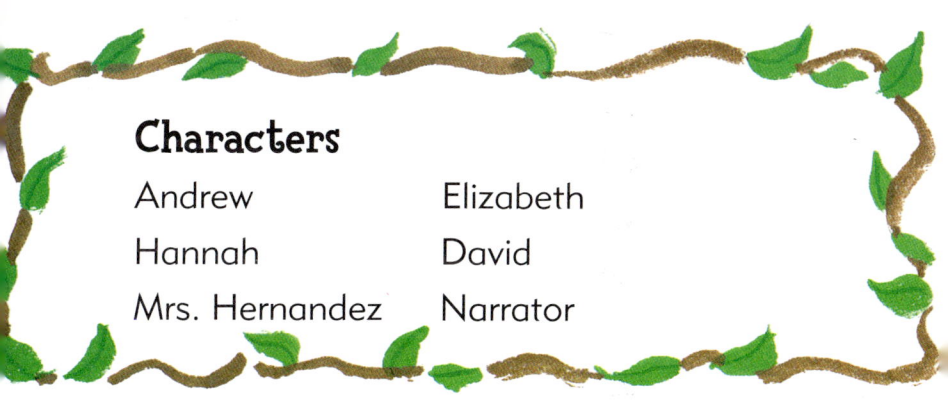

Andrew   Elizabeth
Hannah   David
Mrs. Hernandez   Narrator

Narrator: Andrew, David, Elizabeth, and Hannah are putting on a play. Mrs. Hernandez, their teacher, speaks with them.

Mrs. Hernandez: I love your idea of acting out "Jack and the Bean Stalk." Who can tell me what happens in the play?

David: Jack's family is very poor. His mother sends him to sell the family's cow for money.

Elizabeth: However, Jack doesn't. He meets an old man on the way to town. Jack sells the cow to the man for three "special" beans.

Hannah: Jack gives his mother the beans, and she becomes upset. Jack tells her the beans are special. She won't listen to him. She tosses the beans onto the ground!

Andrew: The next day, the beans have sprouted and grown into a huge bean stalk. Jack climbs the bean stalk. He meets a giant at the top. This giant wants to eat Jack.

David: The giant's wife hides Jack. Jack steals the giant's hen that lays golden eggs.

Elizabeth: Jack climbs back down the bean stalk. The giant climbs down, chasing him.

David: When Jack reaches the bottom of the bean stalk, he cuts it down. The giant falls. Jack is lucky to escape.

Mrs. Hernandez: Good job! Everyone knows the story. Now I would like you to write what the characters will say to each other. That's called the dialogue.

Narrator: The four children take turns suggesting the dialogue that the characters should say. Andrew writes the lines in a notebook. When everyone is satisfied with the lines, they decide they are finished.

Hannah: Let's read through the lines!

David: Okay, but I want to be the giant! I get to say, "Fee, fi, fo, fum!"

Andrew: If you are the giant, I want to be Jack! I'll steal your hen and cut down the bean stalk!

Hannah: I will be Jack's mother. Elizabeth can be the giant's wife.

Narrator: Mrs. Hernandez walks over.

Mrs. Hernandez: Have you all decided who will be in the cast?

Elizabeth: Yes. Would you like to hear us read our lines, Mrs. Hernandez?

Mrs. Hernandez: Yes. Now remember to read the dialogue like your character would really speak. It's important for the dialogue to sound natural.

Andrew: What do I do if my character feels scared or angry?

Mrs. Hernandez: Say your lines with drama! Show the fear in your voice. Let us hear the anger!

Narrator: The children read the lines of the play to their teacher.

Mrs. Hernandez: That was a really great reading!

David: Are we finished with our play project now?

Mrs. Hernandez: Absolutely not! You have to gather your props.

Andrew: Do you mean the special beans? We could make them out of modeling clay.

Elizabeth: We will also need to build a bean stalk! Maybe we could make that out of rope.

Mrs. Hernandez: You have great ideas. What else will the characters need?

Hannah: We have to have a hen and some golden eggs.

Narrator: The group makes a bean stalk out of a climbing rope from the gymnasium. They add a yellow beak to a stuffed white teddy bear so that it looks like a white hen. They make golden eggs out of foil. They also paint the eggs yellow.

Mrs. Hernandez: You are almost finished with your project. What do you think is missing?

Elizabeth: I think we need scenery!

Mrs. Hernandez: We have large sheets of white paper, paint, and paintbrushes in the back of the classroom. What scenery do you wish to paint?

Andrew: We need the outside of Jack's house where he speaks with his mother. That is also where the bean stalk grows.

Hannah: We also need to paint the inside of the giant's house. This is where he keeps the hen and golden eggs.

Narrator: The four children paint the scenery. Then the group gathers to rehearse the play.

Mrs. Hernandez: Now you are ready to rehearse your lines. Can any of you say your lines without reading them?

Hannah, Andrew, David and Elizabeth: Not yet!

Mrs. Hernandez: You need to practice your lines over and over to memorize them. Sometimes practicing in front of a mirror helps.

Narrator: It is the day of the play. The actors put on their costumes. Everyone is ready to perform on the stage except Andrew.

Andrew: I'm so nervous! What if I forget all my lines or trip over my feet? What if the play is a huge disaster?

Hannah: Andrew, don't worry so much. You know your lines better than any of us. There is no reason for you to have stage fright.

David: Hannah is right, Andrew. We've rehearsed the play many times. We are ready!

Narrator: The cast of "Jack and the Bean Stalk" does a wonderful job. The audience claps loudly when the play is over.

Hannah: Putting on that play was really fun.

Andrew: When can we do it again?

Mrs. Hernandez: First, you will have to write another play!

Elizabeth: We need to get some new ideas!

David: All right! Let's get busy! We have a lot of work to do!

Scaffolded Language Development

USING PUNCTUATION On the board, write these sentences from the story:

Who can tell me what happens in the play? *(page 3)*
She tosses the beans onto the ground! *(page 4)*

Draw students' attention to the end punctuation. Point out that the first sentence is a question. Questions are punctuated with a question mark. The second sentence is an exclamation. Exclamations are punctuated with an exclamation point. Read each sentence and have students repeat the sentence chorally with the proper intonation.

Have students copy each of the following sentences and place an exclamation point or question mark as appropriate. Ask students to chorally read the completed sentences.

1. You'd better be careful
2. What a beautiful day
3. What time does the play start
4. Did you memorize all your lines
5. It's time to go

🍎 Health

Growing Beans Have students research the health benefits of eating beans. Have them make a poster to show how beans can be part of a healthy diet.

School-Home Connection

Favorite Stories Have students discuss with a family member what his or her favorite stories are.

Word Count: 866